THE PLURI SOCIETY

SHERRY NING

To those with a sneaking suspicion that they
were meant for more.

The Pluri Society · *noun*

[the plur-ee suh-sai-uh-tee]

The way of life of those who are creative, aspirational, purposeful, and bold enough to dream of everything they could be.

No. 1

Have faith and don't be afraid to dream.

You can aim, but you might miss. You might struggle, lose something valuable, or even fail to capture the dream completely.

But there's one thing worse than any of that: not having a dream at all. To dream means to aim for something you know might not come true, and that alone is enough to scare many of us into a pacified life of quiet obedience.

Feeling like you're meant to do more in life is your signal to do that. Faith is not the absent of doubt—in fact, faith requires doubt because it's the act of going forward even when you don't see the next step with absolute clarity.

Taking the first step is the hardest part. An ounce of faith is often enough to trigger a series of miraculous accomplishments.

Have faith in your prosperity and go build your calling. Life doesn't happen *to* you, but *for* you.

No. 2

You're the captain of your ship. Don't just sail, steer.

Ten years from now, you need to be able to say that this is the life you chose, not the one you settled for.

A future that is created with intention, desire, and deliberation is more fulfilling than one that is scrapped together by avoidance-driven choices.

Be driven by purpose, conviction, and passion, not fear.

No. 3

Build the future you want with longevity in mind.

Short-termism is the defect of modern convenience. We rush. We want things fast at the expense of beauty and significance. We hardly think about our grandchildren's grandchildren's grandchildren's grandchildren when we create something new.

There is a deep virtue in pursuing things that are meaningful and not just instantly satisfying. Doing what's meaningful is not a luxury, it's essential. Doing things with long-term vision should be the default.

No. 4

Keep your heart set on the truth.

Don't compromise your core values to fit in with others. The road to hell is paved with the acceptance of things that inescapably go against your conscience.

Violating what you believe in is a form of self-mockery. Have some faith. Hold on to the truth and keep your vision clear. The one person you can't lie to is yourself.

No. 5

Be somebody who makes everybody feel like a somebody.

The best conversations are the ones where you remember few specific details that anyone said, but have an unforgettably strong, positive, and durable impression of the person overall.

People forget what you say or do but they'll never forget how you made them feel.

Your spark will forever be remembered and cherished; a candle loses nothing by lighting another candle.

No. 6

Have strong preferences.

Never compromise the truth for the sake of popularity, appealing to the norm, or getting along with people who can only get along when they agree.

The more you uphold your values, the more alone you'll feel. Being intentional about the energy you surround yourself with means eliminating what you used to settle for out of a fear of scarcity.

Curate your circle carefully; this is the highest form of self-respect.

Addendum: "Do not conform to the pattern of this world, but be transformed by the renewing of your mind." — Romans 12:2

No. 7

Act as if what you do makes a difference.

Life is remembered by the peaks and troughs, but it's experienced through the in-between moments. The mundane, the routines, the chitchats, the habits.

Every little action matters; don't underestimate your impact. Choices will accumulate and their consequences will compound.

That's why you should always act as if your actions make a difference, because they do.

No matter how little.

No. 8

Don't just exist—live.

Human flourishing roots in the pursuit of meaning, not the maximization of hedonistic experiences. General wellness is not the total amelioration of suffering but the repurposing and transformation of it.

A ship that never sails will never risk being engulf by the storm, but that's not what ships were built for. Living—not just existing— requires a certain toughness.

No. 9

Reward yourself.

Only give the best of yourself when what you're doing is going to give you a better self.

If you don't look back on where you've been, you won't know where you are going. Remember what great misconceptions you once had? What problems you thought were impossible to solve but eventually overcame? Remember how many versions of yourself you've had to leave behind in pursuit of something better? How many mental paradigms have shifted since your Day One?

Remember where you came from and notice how far you've made it—no part of that journey is too small to be celebrated. Be proud of how far you've come and reward yourself.

No. 10

Take some risks.

When Prometheus stole fire from the gods, he was condemned to eternal torment: his liver would be feasted on by a falcon during the day, then, it would grow back at night, only to be eaten again the following morning.

To improve the lives of man, Prometheus took that risk. After all, what makes man different from the animals if not the desire to innovate, bring new ways to his generation, and, in Adam Smith's words, "better his own condition"? What makes our world go round if not the desire to be better off than who we were yesterday?

The path to creating something is difficult and full of risks. But the risk of venture has clearly not deterred everyone from creating new and better ways of living—certainly not Prometheus. Certainly not the engineers who designed the light fixture above your head or the stove that cooks your dinner. Certainly not the thinkers who invented the languages and mathematics that you use. Certainly not the pioneers who developed the machines that make your keys, shoelaces, cars, and eyeglasses.

Everything we depend on came from members of our own species who took risks and stole fire from the gods.

So, cherish your freedom and do the thing you want to do. The greatest risk is not taking any at all. You will never escape the threat of adversity, but you have the right to contend with it.

No. 11

Be competitive (it helps you grow).

The more you compete in something, the more you become like your opponent. Rivalry is resistance—we adapt to the fighting style we're exposed to.

In Nietzsche's words, "Be careful who you choose as your enemy because that's who you become most like."

No. 12

The ordinary life can be a good life.

Introspective people worry the most about falling to mediocrity because, to them, it's the equivalent of being comatose and incapable of independent thinking. But this same group of "gifted" people are also the ones who seem to be fated with an incurable sense of loneliness.

The fear of mediocrity is the fear of being unaware of the passing of time. It's the extreme awareness of *memento mori*. The disdain for mediocrity is the fear that one doesn't really live his own life but is dragged by it.

Do not fall in love with unnecessary suffering—that is a true tragedy. It's good to be a sovereign individual and strive for excellence, but remember that the search for purpose is not supposed to torment you.

No. 13

Always be optimistic.

Beliefs shape subjective reality in a way that is as natural as gravity shapes objective reality.

To manifest, pray, wish, etc. is quite literally alchemy—it's not just a metaphor. Positive expectations invite the Good. Optimism turns the mundane into gold. Manifestation is optimism in motion. Fortune favors those who believe they deserve it and are ready for it.

The future is changed by people who believe they can, because belief is what turns intentions into reality.

As Henry Ford once said, "Whether you think you can or can't, you're right."

No. 14

To understand the word around you, observe its patterns.

We are story-based by nature, we make sense of the world in narratives. The world of material becomes meaningful when we know what we're doing with it (instead of just existing in it).

Just like how non-fiction books study objective reality, fiction studies pragmatic reality. Math and logic tell us what there is, fairytales and mythology tell us what to do with what there is.

Heroes teach us how to live just as much as science experiments.

Pay close attention to the patterns you live among to understand what's going on and to predict what will happen next.

No. 15

Take care of your emotions spiritually.

"It's just chemicals and electricity" is a tragically lifeless reduction of the divine range of human emotions.

Have you ever been in love? Felt seething rage? Burst with jealousy? Been flattened by guilt? Possessed by ecstasy? Had a gut feeling so strong you could've sworn it was from above?

And even if it were just a bunch of chemicals and electricity, what makes you think that *that's* not miraculous?

As the saying goes, "we are not human beings having a spiritual existence, we are spiritual beings having a human experience."

You do not *have* a soul. You *are* a soul, and you have a body.

No. 16

Learn to have fun.

The ultimate charm for anyone in any situation is fun.

People are attracted to fun like moths to a flame. If you can't loosen up, take things less seriously, and occasionally laugh at yourself, it doesn't matter how many interesting things you bring to the table.

No. 17

Watch what you put inside your mind.

We call it "paying" attention because there's a cost to consumption.

Be careful of what you're spending your attention on—it makes up what you think, what you believe in, and who you are.

Take control of what you consume, or the world will take control of who you become.

No. 18

To be original, look for ways to recombine what already exists.

To create is to recombine.

Technologies form by the crossbreeding of existing technologies (e.g., the internet is the offspring of the telephone and the computer). Henry Ford once said, "I invented nothing new. I simply assembled the discoveries of other men behind whom were centuries of work."

There's no such thing as a new idea—ideas come from combinations of existing ideas. Look for ways to create with what is already presented to you.

We can think of the total amount of ideas in the universe as being a constant. We've held the same principles and fantasies throughout time and culture, we've told the same stories over and over again, just in different forms.

No. 19

Enjoy solitude and find yourself in it.

A common reason why we fear solitude is because we fear the possibility of losing our sense of self if left alone for too long.

Much of how we define ourselves is relative to our social circle, and without an object of reference, we'd have no relational orientation.

But solitude is also what it takes to find yourself. Who you are when no one is watching tells you more about who you truly are and what you truly want.

Many people suffer from "the fear of finding oneself alone," remarks André Gide, "and so they don't find themselves at all."

Ground yourself in solitude because if you are everywhere, then you are nowhere.

No. 20

Control your desires.

If you don't know what you want, the world will tell you and you will spend your life chasing meaningless desires that have no value other than what the herd says it is worth.

If you don't control your desires, they will control you and you'll wonder why you're never satisfied.

No. 21

Don't dwell too long on past achievements.

There comes a time when past accomplishments get used up. Beyond that point it starts holding you back.

Treat it as past practice.

Keep on moving forward.

The best is still ahead.

Accomplishments should be your confidence, not a place for you to remain stagnant. The best you'll ever do is still ahead of you, waiting for you to catch up.

No. 22

Find purpose by acting more and thinking less.

Purpose is found through doing, not thinking.

Reality is like memory foam: if you push it, it pushes back in your own contour. That's why we discover ourselves through doing. Our form is defined through actions.

Power is increased through resistance. Want to be stronger? Train harder. Want to be a better writer? Write more. Want to be a better orator? Speak up.

Find something challenging and get as good as you possibly can at it. Do something or the sense of wanting to improve. Feel where your limits are. Find something worthy of struggle and really give it a go.

No. 23

Always live in the present.

Cultivate the ability to utterly erase negative emotions as soon as they start to grow and immediately take the next second as a new life.

Everything you want to do and be is on the other side of fear (of failure and criticism).

Every present moment is the only window in which you are allowed to change.

No. 24

Do what transforms you, not what feels good temporarily.

In times of hardship, it's nearly impossible to believe that the purpose of living is just to pursue happiness.

If the condition of life is to suffer, then our true purpose is to do what is meaningful to us despite this condition. It's not the maximization of positive emotions that produces well-being, but undergoing purposeful challenges that are worthy of us.

No. 25

Have a sense of humor.

It disarms threats. It's the antidote to stuffy and awkward situations. It recovers you from embarrassment. People can be phony, words can get misinterpreted, and the world can be draining.

If you can let things pass with lightness, you'll never stay down for long.

No. 26

Do what empowers you.

Happiness is not to be pursued; it ensues.

When you do what you love and work hard at your passion, challenges suddenly feel worthy of how difficult they are.

When you do things that empower you, happiness follows.

No. 27

Believe in magic.

Magic is not about the supernatural. Magic happens everyday for those who believe in it—miracles happen to those who expect it.

The ability to tell stories with eye contact? The rosiness that grows in your chest when you hug your parents? Those sudden moments of clarity where everything just makes sense like you're seeing yourself from above?

That's magic.

Life is full of it; you just have to choose to see it.

No. 28

Be encouraging.

Being the devil's advocate isn't always what is needed in the moment. Sometimes, people just need a bold vote of confidence, inspiration, and proof of support.

Optimism is infectious—it's a force of good, why not spread it? You only stand to gain.

No. 29

Keep the promises you make to yourself.

One way to build up confidence is by keeping promises you make to yourself.

If you always let yourself down, you'll start feeling like there's nothing stable to depend on internally. Confidence boils down to having trust in your own abilities.

That's the antidote to insecurity.

You are your own closest friend, if you can't even be there for you, how could you possibly think you're reliable? Keeping a promise you've made to yourself builds a sense of security—the first person who can benefit from your ability to deliver and achieve is you.

No. 30

Pursue purpose, not fame.

Put yourself out there because you have something to share, not because you want to be famous. Fame is the excrement of good work. Mike Myers calls it "the industrial disease of creativity."

Your work must be meaningful to you before it is worthwhile for anyone else. Fame, at most, should be the byproduct of truly valuable output.

No. 31

Take advantage of your abundance.

We are rich in potential and optionality. Manifestation is the transmutation of using what you have to turn reality into what you want.

The dots are all there, and they always have been. How they connect is up to you.

You have everything you need—you just need to rearrange them in a way that is useful for you and use them to your advantage.

No. 32

Be your true self.

You know what you are best at? That no one can beat you at? Being you.

Recognize your insecurities and become what you are afraid to be. The undesirable circumstances of today do not have to be the arbitrary limits of tomorrow—take control of your destiny.

As Carl Jung once said, "The privilege of a lifetime is to become who you truly are." Not who you *think* you should be or who others would like you to be, but who you truly are.

No. 33

Dissolve the rigid dichotomy between work and play.

The best work should feel like play because it should come naturally to you, and the best play should be productive because it's a form of experiential learning.

We usually see things that are "productive" as work (usually measured by income), and everything else as frivolous. But play is serious work. How we play is how we learn to act and think. Montessori once said, "The hands are the instruments of man's intelligence."

Work should be a natural extension of your innate tendency for action: if left to your own devices, what do you naturally start doing? What do you want and like to do?

Take play seriously.

No. 34

Use placebo as your superpower.

"It's all just psychological conditioning"—so what? Isn't it pretty advantageous to get what you want just by believing in it?

There's a reason why good things happen to people who believe they deserve it. Faith is a very tangible thing, don't overlook it.

No. 35

Know what you want (and why).

It's difficult but necessary to know what you want.

The first step in achieving big dreams is just having the courage to want things that you know are very challenging but worthy of achieving. If you want something you have to first believe that it exists and that it's humanly possible to obtain it.

Why does it take courage to want? Why are we scared of dreaming big?

Because as soon as we've determined what we think of as "successful", we've also determined what we think of as "unsuccessful". That's why it's so difficult to set goals. So, we become scared of pursuing what we want because of the fear of failing. The question is, would you rather fail in actuality or succeed in mere theory?

The best way to never fail is to not have any goals set in the first place—it's easier to just dream smaller.

No. 36

Distinguish money-problems from non-money-problems.

When people say money buys happiness, they mean that money solves problems and reduces inconveniences. But, at the end of the day, money only solves problems that money can solve.

Passion can't be fueled by paper. Dreams can't be purchased with any currency other than belief and will. Every mistake, no matter how costly, can bring you incredible profit if you learn from it. The freedom to pursue what you want is true fortune, and doing so without worrying what others think of you is true wealth. Let dignity and morale be your net worth.

True fulfillment is bought with earnestness, joy, and compassion. Do anything with love and it will bring a salary of a life worth living.

No. 37

Look for compatibility in all your relationships.

Compatibility is the key to everything: what you do for a living, who you date, where you choose to live, and so on. The word "compatible" comes from *compati*, Latin for "to suffer with".

Date someone you're able to go through hardships with.

Work a job you're willing to pull late nights for because it suits you.

So on.

As the saying goes, "when there's a will, there's a way."

No. 38

Notice where your desires come from.

We become the average of the people we spend the most time with. Gradually, we adopt their beliefs, their mannerisms, their ideas, and their desires.

We want what our friends want; this is known as mimetic theory.

"People don't have original thoughts" isn't the most useful takeaway from mimetic theory. The real lesson here is that because most of our desires root in imitation, we ought to surround ourselves with good influence.

Live and consume selectively.

No. 39

Avoid these things that bring general unhappiness:

- Worrying about things that haven't happened yet or can't be changed.
- Needing everyone to agree with you.
- Believing that personal gain must require crushing others.
- Not being able to tell what's trivial and arguing over small things.

No. 40

If your mind needs:

Nourishment—read.

Cardio—write.

Resistance training—debate.

Clarity—meditate.

Relaxation—exercise.

Rest—sleep.

Comfort—pray.

No. 41

To write well, say more with less.

Write poorly and they remember the writer, write wonderfully and they remember the story.

Writing is the packaging of ideas. Good writing delivers ideas to readers. Great writing makes readers think they came up with the ideas themselves.

Great writing taps into the reader's subconscious and articulates for them what they already think. That's the aha-moment.

Effective writing is the arbitrage of capturing what people already think before they realize it themselves. People only resonate with writing when it speaks to a part of them that already exists. In fact, good writing should flow like water. Every word must serve the purpose of leading to the next. One sentence to the next, one page to the next. Be continuous, but also be concise; do not waste words.

Good writers say more with less. Good books are over before you even know it.

No. 42

Be more disciplined.

Discipline will get you places motivation can't.

There is no secret to "making it". It just boils down to the power of consistency and compounding. Do something well and do it over

and

over

and

over

again.

No. 43

Rekindle your childlike wonder.

Re-reading fairytales and fables with grown-up eyes is a very soothing and humbling experience.

All grown-ups were once children...but only few of them remember it. Innocence can teach so much about the most profound meanings of love and life. Things like "follow your heart", "don't bottle up your emotions", or "appreciate the small things and live in the moment" don't truly register until you realize how much of your childlike wonder has been lost along the way.

No. 44

Do things with love.

Take cooking, for example. The mood and mentality of the cook changes the quality of the dish. That's why mother's cooking tastes different. There is love in her work. Her secret ingredient is care.

Do things with genuine care. Use your heart.

When someone uses their love in their craft, their creation is different.

No. 45

Finish what you start.

When you work on something you're passionate about, you look past the drudgery, time, and cost. That's because when you work on something you love, you only see the end product. You see the best possible outcome, not its current progress. You see what it could be, not what it is right now.

But, more often than not, plans get thwarted, goals get updated, and the final product can end up drastically different from what was imagined.

Many of these changes are not in our control; fate can be a thief of dreams.

However, even if we don't get to control how something ends, we can control *if* and *when* it ends.

No matter how your plans end, make sure it's at the place where there is nothing left for you to do, not where you gave up.

No matter where you are, the choice to give up or finish what you start is always yours to make.

No. 46

If you won't care about it on your deathbed, don't worry too much about it.

This may sound morbid, but every time you feel anxious about something, imagine yourself on your deathbed reminiscing on that thing as if it were a memory of the past and ask yourself, "do I, in these final moments, care about that thing from back then?"

The anxiety usually fades.

No. 47

Add by subtracting.

Michelangelo famously said, "The sculpture is already complete within the marble block, before I start my work. It is already there; I just have to chisel away the superfluous material."

What you are looking for may be hidden, but it certainly isn't hiding from you. All the potential you will ever have is already inside you.

Do more and think less. Eliminate what isn't supposed to be there and reveal what is. The masterpiece will remain forever trapped inside the slab of marble if you never subtract.

No. 48

Feel your emotions, don't avoid them.

If you want to "get over" something, you need to go through it entirely instead of avoiding it. Befriend your emotions and feel them completely.

As Freud says, "Unexpressed emotions will never die. They are buried alive and will come forth later in uglier ways."

No. 49

Pay attention to your fears.

Fear reveals what you care about.

For example, people-pleasing is often motivated by the fear of disappointing others.

What this reveals about the people-pleaser is that they care deeply about being liked, feeling useful, or being needed.

No. 50

Embrace your spirituality.

Therapy is not healing unless there's a spiritual dimension to it.

"Psyche" means soul in Greek; psychology was never meant to be secular. This might not refer to organized religion, but there has to be elements of divinity, transcendence, and eternity.

No. 51

Be like water.

Lean into the shape of your container, don't be afraid to take up space. Work with gravity, let it accelerate your movement. Flow around obstacles, be flexible. Flow around people, forgive frictions and disagreements. You can be gentle and powerful at the same time.

No. 52

Be decisive.

It is ridiculously underrated how important it is to be confident and decisive about what you like and don't like.

As Cicero said, "More is lost by indecision than wrong decision."

Being decisive forces you to face the reality that there will always be a mismatch between the amount of information available and the information you need. Get comfortable acting with incomplete information. Get used to not being in control of results.

The moment of decision is what determines if you can hold your ground or be swept away by the overwhelming possibilities.

Being decisive forces you to become something.

No. 53

Read more fiction.

Stories help us make sense of the world. We are the characters in the ongoing narrative of history. Fiction is a map of meaning, it's a description of the world as it signifies for action.

And that's way more helpful than non-fiction self-help.

No. 54

Do not look outside yourself for approval.

Lovelessness is the biggest cause of insecurity. If you've never been properly loved before, your identity becomes a prisoner of other's judgments. When they laugh at our jokes, we're confident that we're likeable. If they roll their eyes, we fall into a spiral of self-doubt.

This is why a majority of self-help psychology is centered around self-discovery: our deepest desire is to be free from the pointing, nagging, and insincere smooching of the world by becoming a fair assessor of our own strengths and weaknesses.

When someone is properly grounded in life, they shouldn't have to look outside themselves for approval.

No. 55

Add more beauty.

One of the most important lessons my mother ever taught me is that all things must be done with beauty. Eating is not just about nutrition, plating matters. Writing is not just thought-dumping, eloquence matters. Dressing is not just fashion and function, style matters.

Beauty is not just decorative, it is vital.

Minimalism done for the sake of "aesthetics" (as opposed to a genuine philosophy of living with less) is ugly. It's the emperor's new clothes. It's boring and sterile. It lacks life, color, identity, and taste. You don't always need opulence, but you always need personality.

Sometimes, more is more.

No. 56

Recognize your vulnerability.

The fact that being seen naked in front of a crowd is a common nightmare shows how primal our understanding of vulnerability is. It applies to both mind *and* body. To be naked, physically *and* figuratively, is to be embarrassed, ashamed, and mercilessly exposed with nowhere to hide.

But this is what distinguishes man from beast; the recognition of your own vulnerability is what makes a human animal a person.

No. 57

Don't be insulted by disrespect.

Criticism and disrespect are forms of flattery. If you truly didn't like something, you wouldn't bother giving it your time and attention to explain why you didn't like it. Indifference is the ultimate insult.

No. 58

Practice gratitude and generosity.

Gratitude has this magical ability to make you see how many of the things you take for granted were actually gifted to you not because you deserve it but because someone was generous. That is grace and it is the core tenet of Christianity:

Grace describes someone who is gifted life despite being despicable, by someone who is perfectly eager to give a life by trading in his own. The result of this ultimate sacrifice demands that instead of feeling indebted or guilty, the saved sinner could be inspired by such grace to also be generous, creating a domino effect and spreading grace. Hence, the word "Christian" means to be Christ-like.

We don't focus on this principle much in secular society because there's usually profit incentive. But that doesn't cancel out the fact that someone still had to sacrifice their time to provide us with a good or service. For example, we should still treat waiters as if we were dining for free.

If we look beyond transactions and the expectations of reciprocity, we can focus more on what has been sacrificed and what to truly give our appreciation to.

No. 59

Embrace your talent.

My favorite quote from Naval is, "escape competition through authenticity."

True value is impossible to mimic, either by artificial intelligence or other people. A truly talented person's day will come, in the same way that gold nuggets don't stay hidden in the earth for long.

Don't just do something well, do something you love. Do things that align with your sense of self, do things you don't have to try at. Anyone who tries to copy you will always be one step behind because they'll always need you to make the first move.

If you are meant to do something, it should come easily to you. It doesn't mean that there won't be challenges. It doesn't mean that you should just fall complacent to the path of least resistance. Instead, it means that you should find the path that feels natural and let it accelerate you.

No. 60

Do not lie to yourself.

The one person you absolutely can not lie to is yourself, even if you tried. Accumulated cognitive dissonance makes you lose sight of what is important. Too many lies and eventually you won't know what you care about. You'll lose sight of what is meaningful.

Truth is more of a bitter medicine than a recreational drug, but do you know what hurts more than the truth? Shame. Shame is deforming and will find you no matter where you hide. It's a wound that'll never heal and a scar that'll never fade.

The only weapon that can drive out shame is honesty. And anything that can be formulated with words can be conquered with compassion and forgiveness.

No. 61

Focus on building your skills.

To college students, I would advise you to focus on building your skills and figuring out what value you can bring to your peers with your unique obsession or passion.

Networks are the byproduct of good work—do good things and naturally the journey will be filled with good people.

No. 62

Don't try to change others.

People are like pottery clay: easily shaped
while they're young and malleable. Under
different hands, the same mud can become a
vase or a mug or a plate or a pendant. But try
to change them after they've dried and
hardened and they shatter into pieces.

No. 63

Be humble and admit it when you're stumped.

You can be well-liked even if you're associated with controversial figures by playing the role of the fool. Be humble and assume that the person you're talking to knows something that you don't.

Make everybody feel good about being themselves. Be somebody who makes everybody feel like a somebody by paying genuine interest in what they're expressing.

Be humble and admit it when you don't understand something. Entertains ideas without accepting, condemning, or worshipping them.

Be the type of person who can chat with anyone, from a first grader to a graduate researcher. This kind of social skill makes you super likeable because it shows that you're secure and not blinded by a need for status or superiority.

No. 64

Express love in the small things.

Love is found in the everyday actions that say, "I know you and I care about you."

They make your morning coffee just the way you like it, they chase you to the door because you forgot your gloves on a cold day, they make you walk on the inside of the sidewalk… things like that.

No. 65

Watch your thoughts, they show on your face.

Nature gives you your face at twenty but the face you have at forty is the one you deserve. Your face imprints your thoughts, feelings, and expressions.

Imagine a cynic, for example. Being cynical makes you scowl, and if you scowl too frequently your face will permanently look like you're ready to complain.

Pinocchio is a genius representation of how it feels inside when you lie. Lies are distortions of reality, a twist on the truth. If you never smoothen it out, the lie just keeps growing and twisting until it becomes so unignorable and burdensome it shows on your face.

No. 66

Strive to win.

Are you aiming for the best or just "good enough"?

You need to want to win.

Participation-trophy culture discourages excellence—*outcomes don't matter, just enjoy the journey*. But being hungry for victory is a birthright. Ambition is morally virtuous. You should want the best for yourself.

No. 67

Help those who are younger than you or those who are currently at where you once were.

We feel compelled to mentor people who remind us of our younger selves because wanting the best for them feels like wanting the best for ourselves.

The advice we give them are usually things we wish we had heard earlier. I enjoy chatting with peers from my alma mater, but I feel the urge to help them more unconditionally when I see myself in them. There's a subconscious curiosity that wants to living vicariously through them by making decisions again at their age.

This tells us one other thing: we should strive to be the person our younger self wanted but never had.

No. 68

Have some integrity.

We've all heard of the adage, "actions matter more than words."

And it's true—your words are only as powerful as the actions they precede. What you say matters. But if you don't follow through, you rob your words of their value.

The world of unfulfilled commitments is artificial. It's the place where people only say what others want to hear. It's where people pretend to be responsible for what they know they can't avoid.

Good intentions are nothing but an illusion until you choose to fulfill them.

No. 69

Catch up with old friends.

Catching up with old friends that you used to see everyday is like an archeological excavation of your own character development because they dig up an older version of yourself that's been buried with time. Your past self resurfaces as you interact with them again.

Hanging out with old friends who haven't changed is one of the best feelings in the world. They bring out a part of you that you thought you outgrew because "life went on".

As we grow, we keep every age inside of us. Younger versions of yourself never truly disappear, they get frozen in memories, and get defrosted by specific people, inside jokes, and places and scents.

No. 70

Make decisions before it's too late.

Decisions are the unit economics of life. Choosing one thing is simultaneously the rejection of all other things.

Diversification is good, but discrimination is necessary.

You must know what you want and act on it. Otherwise, you'll end up with nothing but expired imaginations.

Dan Sullivan's definition of hell is, "your last day on Earth, the person you became meets the person you could have become."

No. 71

Believe in yourself.

"Yea but what if I—" what if you believed in yourself? A single match can burn down a forest. A single quiet realization can dissolve years of pessimism. A single invention can change an industry. You contain more than you lack, so apply your advantage and seize your moment.

A great majority of our limitations are in our heads, not our hands. We suffer more in imagination than reality: when we leverage our strengths at the right time, a small act can redefine everything.

More often, we should be landing firmly on our feet from our leaps of faith.

No. 72

Vet your ideas.

Inside your head is where you spend most of your life. It's where dreams dwell and where thoughts turn into decisions. Carefully vet your mental influences: the music you listen to, the advice you take, and so forth.

Because what happens in your head will shape how you act.

And how you act will shape how you live.

No. 73

Spend your time wisely.

There is no 'right' time, there is only time and how you spend it. An extra hour of scrolling on your phone wouldn't matter if you lived forever. But you don't live forever.

How long are you going to wait before you demand the best for yourself?

People say time goes by, but time says people go by. Time consumes us all and only gives each of us one little piece of itself. And even that is something we must return at the end of everything.

Time is passing. Time waits for no one.

While you play, while you work, while you complain, while you dream, while you wait, time is passing and it will never come back. This moment is already over, but that's not what matters—what matter is whether or not you will seize the next one.

No. 74

Do what is meaningful.

We live in an age of material wealth but
spiritual poverty. The pleasure-oriented
consumerist culture we are immersed in is like
junk food for the soul; we're sick because we're
overfed with shallow entertainment and
starved of the nutrition our meaning-seeking
nature needs.

No. 75

Give back to the village that raised you.

Gratitude is the greatest motivator. Realizing that you stand on the shoulders of giants, that everything you have now was fought and labored for by those who came before you and had way less than you. Nothing gets a person motivated like a deep appreciation for collective prosperity.

As Steve Jobs said, "What drove me? I think most creative people want to express appreciation for being able to take advantage of the work that's been done by others before us. I didn't invent the language or mathematics I use. I make little of my own food, none of my own clothes. Everything I do depends on other members of our species and the shoulders that we stand on."

No. 76

Don't rely on self-help books for answers you already have inside of you.

Things are only a problem if they're a problem.

Not everything needs to be normalized, and not everything is worth agonizing over. Life is more than a series of problems—it's an experience.

Life is more like a craft, less like a standardized procedure. You have to be scrappy sometimes to figure out your personal style and your own way of doing things. Adopt a healthy level of skepticism.

You come into this world equipped with all the remedies you'll ever need, and there will always be more solutions than problems. So, take external advice with a grain of salt and start looking within.

No. 77

Simplify.

Be content with less.

No. 78

Make your own utopia.

The world doesn't lack talent it lacks high-agency talent.

I often think about the intelligent people that ended up in high-paying corporate roles after college, and I think about what they'd be capable of if they had more of a ruthless conviction in something they were passionate about.

The paved path in corporate life has its own difficulties but the pathless path in entrepreneurship or innovation requires much more tenacity and grit.

Don't pursue something just because it's easy; do it because it's meaningful. Being able to create your personal utopia out of indifferent reality is the purest measure of intelligence. Success is just being able to have life the way you want it. Being "smart" is just the ability to get what you want.

No. 79

Know what kind of creative you are.

Consumption-production ratio matters.

For instance, I'm a slow reader and I don't get through many books. But the amount of synthesis and creativity I can generate from a single page is enough to be its own chapter.

High C/P ratio writers are knowledge caches. They make a myriad of references and can dissect a single topic from various perspectives. But, high C/P writers risk not fully digesting what they consume, or not fully understanding or benefiting from their reading.

Low C/P ratio writers are the value writers. They tend to produce evergreen content. Since all their output can be traced to a few inputs, the more they create the closer to get to core axioms, principles, and universal truths. But, low C/P writers are more prone to ideology or close-mindedness.

No. 80

Travel more and expand your horizon.

Proust once said, "The real voyage of discovery consists not in seeking new landscapes but in having new eyes."

Travel to see the world, but also to see the world within—you learn a lot about yourself by being in a foreign place.

We naturally seek familiarity; we look for home and safety everywhere we go. Travelling challenges this; do you get scared when you get lost? Does it frustrate you when no one around you speaks the same language? How many new diets can you stomach? How do you react to an entirely new culture with different etiquettes?

Travelling reveals to you who you are underneath your habits of comfort. Look for new patterns in a new set of dots. Interact with strangers of an opposite culture, people you might never see again. Fall in love with a new city. Find out what you hate. Learn to budget your money, time, and energy.

Travelling is what makes life an adventure.

No. 81

Transform your fears into something great.

Fear is the raw material for inspiration.

First, we're intimated or threatened by something.

Then, we come to understand and empathize with it.

Then, we grow fond of it and what used to scare us awes us.

Overtime, our admiration turns into inspiration and vision.

What causes fear in your heart? I believe that most mental renewals start by clarifying what makes you nervous and unraveling why it makes you feel that way.

If you want a revelation, befriend what you fear.

No. 82

Mind your own business.

There are only two reasons why people don't mind their own business: one, they have no mind, and two, they have no business.

No. 83

Worry less about how others see you.

Stop worrying about what other people think of you. Be proud of your work and don't sell yourself short. People looking for reasons to criticize you will always find it—damned if you do, damned if you don't.

Your accomplishments shouldn't warrant their jealousy: Your success has nothing to do with their failure. Your confidence isn't the cause of their insecurity. Your peace doesn't validate their anger or spite. Be your authentic self and put your genuine self into your work.

As Marcus Aurelius once said, "It never ceases to amaze me: we all love ourselves more than other people, but care more about their opinion than our own."

No. 84

Do more of what makes you feel alive.

Life is as simple as just doing more of what you like and what makes you feel like a more excellent version of yourself, less of what makes you shrivel.

No. 85

Create for the better.

Change must start with love. Want to change someone's mind? They won't care what you know until they know how much you care. Want to change yourself? You must genuinely want the best for yourself; self-hatred can feel like fuel at first but it always leads to self-destruction.

No. 86

Know yourself to make the best decisions.

Knowing yourself is the first step to doing anything great. You have limited resources, time, motivation, but there are nearly no limits to your potential—you can become almost anything, but not everything. Choosing is the hard part. Direction is more important than speed.

You hold an entirely unique and irreplaceable place in the world. You're the sum of a lifetime of experiences. You can be described but you can't be summarized or defined by anyone except you. To know yourself intimately is to know what you're capable of doing with what you have.

Figure out who you want to be and how you want to live before figuring out what you have to do.

No. 87

Seek what inspires you.

Inspiration is different from awe. Standing still in admiration is one thing, feeling compelled to act is another.

Inspiration should bother you, actually—it should feel like a pebble in your shoe, a constant nudge reminding you that you're still far away from your highest.

No. 88

Assess if a decision is necessary before making one.

A lot of times when I start overthinking decisions I zero in on three questions:

1) What do I want?
2) What do I not want?
3) Do I need to make a decision right now?

Getting to the bottom of desires and motivations immediately simplifies the situation.

No. 89

Be flexible.

One of the biggest differences between school and the real world is that the real world is much more malleable, but it's also a lot more eliminatory.

School is about rules, theory, and structure. The real world is about survival. There really are only two types of people in the world: those that learn from mistakes and those that don't. The real world doesn't educate, but it teaches. Whether or not you learn is up to you.

The real world favors those who seize the moment regardless of surrounding chaos: School rewards obedience and the real world rewards curiosity.

School rewards those good at logic; the real world rewards those good with people.

School emphasizes risk management; the real world reveals bigger rewards in risk-taking.

No. 90

Know what you want.

Industrialization led to abundance, which led to choice anxiety. The need to soul-search comes from the floating anxiety of not knowing what we want or where our desires come from.

That's why the next cultural shift will be about being anti-mimetic—that is, living freely by pursuing what we know is meaningful to ourselves.

When we don't know what we want, we end up wanting what everyone else wants. Desires that are decided for us by the world do not fulfill us. The true objective behind it is usually about wanting to impress people who don't even care.

No. 91

Avoid snobbery.

Snobbery is the fear that we will be seen as ignoble if we let our images loose. Snobbery is the blind pride of those overridden with status anxiety, unable to tell what's truly good behind appearances.

Snobbery is the outward expression of one's inner insecurity about how others might see them.

Snobbery is motivated by the fear that if we use the wrong adjective, pick the wrong wine, or identify the wrong composer, our illusory image of nobility will be exposed as a fraud.

What if we judged less and observed more? When we let go of heuristics and become more charitable to what could be instead of what already is.

No. 92

Be a good storyteller.

Great storytellers assume their audience is smart and leave enough room for them to do some of the work. Great storytellers challenge them and reward them with ownership of the experience. Great storytellers allow the audience to form their own opinions.

You want people to see value in your work? To pay attention and make you part of their lifestyles? If you want them to take you seriously, then give them something to be serious about. Don't dumb down your message.

Give it gravity and challenge them to think for themselves.

No. 93

Avoid envy.

It's hard to love thy neighbor because envy strengthens with social proximity. When someone is too like us, admiration sours into rivalry. This is what Aristotle meant by we can't wish for our friends to be gods—when fate favors someone just like, but isn't, us.

This is why we enjoy Schadenfreude (German, 'harm-joy'), which is pleasure at the misfortune of others. Schadenfreude feels sickly delightful because we love hearing about the fall of people we think are "doing too well".

Envy makes people shake their fist at fate and ask 'why not me?' It invites one to indulge in brooding over one's own misery and resentment. Envy breeds hatred and sabotage. It makes you think, 'if I can't have it, no one can.'

The only fruit of envy is destruction. This is why the Bible warns: "Do not gloat when your enemy falls; when he stumbles, do not let your heart rejoice, or the Lord will see and disapprove and turn his wrath away from him" (Proverbs 24:17-18).

No. 94

Transform your pain, don't pretend it never existed.

There's a strange purity-fixated approach to healing. A lot of modern self-help tries to eradicate suffering, undo past behavioral patterns, and dissolve the ego for the sake of disconnecting the self from trauma.

The blank-slate approach is not very helpful: How can suffering be integrated and understood instead of sanitized away from every surface of the human experience? Struggling is what make us human, it's what makes us grow. Well-earned wisdom always comes from past sufferings.

Freud once said, "One day, in retrospect, the years of struggle will strike you as the most beautiful."

No. 95

Move on.

Unlike school, the real world doesn't always have an answer key.

Sometimes, there is no closure—you don't need to know what went wrong; you just have to move on. By dragging the past into the present, you are doing your future a great disservice. You don't need to understand something in order to accept it, and most times in the real world accepting is all you can do.

Knowing when the ship has sailed is more important than why it has sailed.

No. 96

Watch who you are when no one is watching.

Identity is what you describe; sense of self is what you feel.

Identity is how you're seen by others; sense of self is how you're seen by yourself.

Identity is how you answer the question 'tell me about yourself'; sense of self is what you are when no one's watching.

No. 97

Practice to get better.

Practice is like microdosing reality because you can't cheat yourself on how good you truly are at something. It takes a long time to be yourself, let alone the best version of yourself. At the end of the day, the only way to improve is by practicing. There are no shortcuts.

You are not just who you are in the present, you are also holding the potential of who you can become.

You are a being who is constantly becoming, the greatest gift you have in the present is the ability to choose who you want to be next. The Latin aphorism, *ars longa, vita brevis*, describes exactly this: "Skillfulness takes time and life is short."

In order to become anything, you must eliminate everything else—life is about choosing your sacrifices, you don't get to not make any, but you get to choose which ones.

No. 98

Embrace clumsiness.

You know why jazz sounds happy? Because it's free in form. It's meticulous one second then deliberately clumsy the next. It's as silky smooth, punchy, or groovy as it wants to be. It's not only comfortable with the lack of popular musical structure but makes the best out of it. Every 'wrong' note is just the right beginning for the next. Duke Ellington once said, "if it sounds good, it's good."

In life, we often overcomplicate things—if something makes you happy, it makes you happy. There's no need for everyone to 'get' you, you don't have to conform.

As Leo Tolstoy puts it, "If you want to be happy, be."

No. 99

Face your ideals.

Encountering our ideals and facing rejections are experiences that force us to question our own adequacy. Life is a series of these sorts of revelations—to grow, or even just to change, is to be repeatedly confronted with situations that give us clues that we aren't perfect.

No. 100

Sow your seeds for tomorrow.

The fact that my current thoughts are shaped by books I've read 3-6 years ago heavily influences what I choose to read today. Knowledge is food for the mind, even styles can get absorbed. I find myself speaking and writing like the authors I consume the most.

No. 101

Be careful with the way you act.

Reputation is formed on what you've done, not what you say you'll do.

This is because reputation is the byproduct of character. It's the shadow of actions—it can't move or change unless you do.

Reputation is not 'you', it's the projected image of you once it has left your control.

No. 102

Always have hope.

There are three reasons why hope is necessary for success:

1) It makes you prepared. When you believe that it'll happen, you'll be ready for it when it does.
2) It eliminates distractions. Knowing your 'yes' makes it easy to identify all the 'no's.
3) It gives you direction. Having intentional beliefs gives you something to aim at.

Having hope maximizes your chances of getting lucky.

No. 103

Avoid comparison—focus on your own journey.

Whenever I'm envious of someone I ask myself 'would I be willing to switch lives with them?' And 99.9% of the time my answer is no—it's grounding this way because you realize you can't cherry-pick what you want without enduring the parts you don't want.

Most of the time when we complain that life isn't fair, we're really just complaining that our own life isn't perfect. Since we can not become everything in the first place, there is no point in comparing who we are today to who someone else chose to be a long time ago. And since time does not go back, what good does it serve to wonder 'what if'? You and your neighbor have made different sacrifices, you likely lack what they have, but they also likely lack something that you have.

Therefore, do not compare yourself to others.

No. 104

Do things for yourself.

We spend most of our time doing things we hate with people who won't even be at our funeral. Never settle for something you don't like, and stop pretending you like it. Be honest and start choosing.

Your happiness is your own responsibility. Your sense of meaning is your own responsibility. No one can make you more fulfilled than yourself. No one can embark on your journey for you. You have to do it for yourself.

No. 105

Set goals.

Without a why, you'll never find the how. Without a measure, you'll always be wasting resources. Without a destination, you'll end up where you started.

Without goals, you can run as fast as you can and still be in the same place. Without a target, you'll squander your talents and creativity.

You can't always hit your goals, but you won't hit anything if you don't have an aim. Set some goals and take a chance, or be left with nothing.

No. 106

Build.

The default condition of things is chaos because the world is entropic. If left alone, things deteriorate. It takes conscious effort to slow that down, let alone swim upstream and build against it.

To be human is to build against entropy. To be human is to turn indifferent reality into useful and meaningful things. It's to invent, to write, to assemble, and to calculate. It's to build carriages and then upgrade them into cars. It's to engineer planes that go faster, towers that reach higher, and medicines that heal faster.

There is something divine about creating. From building a software to writing a book to completing a self-portrait, every act of creation is a miniature Genesis. Our creations are designed for our usage. We have created technology in our own image. We are the Maker's makers.

To create is to transform what we are given into something of significance—specifically, something that lives into the future long after we are dead. This is what we call a legacy.

No. 107

Nurture your passion.

Passion is closely associated with obsession because it measures your willingness to go all in with no backup plan—but passion isn't blind obsession.

The flames of passion don't consume, they purify. And purification is the intentional elimination of what's unnecessary: This kind of pruning and refining is what makes going all in effective. Obsession is just going down a rabbit hole, it doesn't promise any great accomplishments.

The active precision and attentiveness of passion is what makes obsession a powerful tool for doing great things.

No. 108

Do what you love.

We are sentimental beings. We want to be something more than we want to have something.

What matters to us at the end of the day is our sense of fulfillment—and that's a reward only given to the passionate, the conscientious, and the dedicated. Getting this reward is no trivial accomplishment.

Don't throw away your dreams thinking that the condition is that it must give you something in return. If it's conditional, it's not love.

Do not let external desperation wipe out the internal drive. Go all-or-nothing. Do what you love.

No. 109

Who you spend time with determines who you become.

Relationships are mutually conditioning: you're the Pavlov to their Dog and vice versa. Their habits cause your reactions until those repeated reactions become *your* habits. And vice versa.

Albert Einstein's theory of general relativity is the theory of gravity. It's the fundamental idea that instead of being an invisible force that attracts objects to one another, gravity is a curving of space and changes with mass. Things don't have an innate ability to attract; the movement between two objects affect them mutually with their respective masses and the distance between them.

The psychological connections we have with each other is as tangible as the physical. Our relationships are determined by the distance of our intimacy and the masses of our individual soulfulness, self-awareness, and ability to love. Like celestial bodies, the gravity that forms between us describes our identities.

No. 110

Watch your thoughts, they become your character.

I don't think people take the space inside their heads seriously enough. The mind is a very sacred place—it's where beliefs grow. And beliefs are powerful. Every cell in your body eavesdrops on your thoughts, your beliefs are the starting point of what you do and who you become.

Vet carefully.

This is what Voltaire meant by "one must cultivate one's own garden." Keep a good distance between what's in your head and what's in the world—you don't need to take interest in every political issue or every petty argument. Pay attention to what brings you peace and do more of that.

No. 111

Meet your heroes.

It's both anticlimactic and daunting to realize that your heroes are only human. It means they once stood where you are now. It means you can take their place. The people you look up to are not that much smarter than you, you can set your own pace and carve out your own path.

External expectations start mattering less when you set your own standards. Even failures feel like a source of pride when it happens on your own terms.

Don't work to please public demand—your work is only as worthwhile to others as it is meaningful to yourself.

No. 112

Find your stillness.

Everyone needs a method of cultivating extreme stillness. It's the only state of being that produces good decisions. Epiphanies and sudden moments of clarity are all born from periods of intense peace; the whispers of intuition can only be heard when your mental space is silent.

No. 113

Have the courage to want and believe that you deserve it.

There's nothing better than being able to plan like an adult yet want like a child.

Abraham Maslow called this the "impulse voice", which is the voice inside a child that tells them what they want. *I want this candy. I don't want that toy. I like this, I hate that.* It's primitive and pre-verbal.

Although it's important for us to learn how to control our impulses as we age, we may have accidently silenced the immense wisdom hidden in these instincts. One way to reconnect with your most primal self is to find out what it is that you loved doing as a child.

The first step to getting what you want is believing that you deserve it—this is what children do best. The benefit of impulsive desires is that they make you so optimistic that you act as if success is inevitable.

Have the courage to want what you want; it's ridiculously simple yet so easily overlooked.

No. 114

Know where your boundaries are and learn to say no.

Consider twice before you accept someone else's responsibility.

Don't let your insecurity become someone else's easy satisfaction. Knowing your boundaries is good for them as much as it is good for you.

Don't become someone else's easy way out. Would you rather be liked now or respected in the future?

No. 115

Play the hand you're dealt.

Water floats a boat when it's on the outside but sinks the boat when it gets on the inside. Circumstances are neutral; it's the way we use it that determines what will make or break us. Play the hand you're dealt. Make your own luck.

No. 116

Be careful of self-sabotage.

The perpetual consumption of self-help content is a form of mental obesity. Self-help can be good knowledge, but if you're not doing anything with what you learn, you're doing yourself a disservice by creating the illusion that you're "improving". Action will always beat consumption when consumption is never digested.

The truth about growth is that there's a part of you that works hard to prevent change, because what's familiar is what's safe. Deep down inside there's a craving for stagnation because it means you won't ever be challenged.

Self-help feels good because we'd rather challenge ourselves in imagination than in reality. It's easy to intellectualize growth and change but to actually do something about it is very hard. It's easy to self-sabotage then rationalize it with 'I guess I didn't deserve it.'

Everyone wants to change for the better but some people want it so bad they act on it.

Small difference, huge leap.

No. 117

Be the change you want to see.

Memos like "be the change you want to see in the world" and "change starts with you" sound corny but it really just means that taking care of yourself *is* taking care of others.

When you change, it affects everyone around you, then everyone around them—no one exists in isolation. Change really does start from you. It's the least you can do because, well, you don't want to pull everyone else down, but it's also the most you can do because you can't change others, you only have control over yourself.

I take care of me for you, you take care of you for me. Do not underestimate how important you are to those who love and care about you, you take up an irreplaceable seat in the world.

No. 118

Ask good questions.

Never suppress your desire to learn. Appearing stupid is still smarter than appearing ignorant.

Those who don't have the patience to answer your question are only insecure about their own competency and struggle for knowledge.

No. 119

Be a good person.

Don't forget to have fun—treat things as play.
Don't forget that the finish line is the same for
everyone. At your funeral, would you want to
be remembered as a 'fast-learner' or as
someone who was generous and kind? Some
virtues are for resumes, others are for life.

No. 120

Think independently before joining discourse.

Great minds think alike because all the ideas that will ever exist already exist. Great thinkers are bound to arrive at the same destination (i.e., objective truths). Great minds are bound to realize the same things from first principles.

No. 121

Always try your best.

You know who never fails? People who never try. If you stand up for something, you're going to meet resistance and get knocked down a few times. You've failed before? Good, it means you're motivated and you've got stamina. Let failure be a measure of your conviction and passion.

No. 122

Be resilient.

Strength is a seed planted deeply within you that has to be fertilized with challenging yet meaningful experiences to break through the surface of your being.

Sorrow and struggle are the water for your soul, but it'll never help you grow if you don't let it seep into you. It must reach places where light has never graced, because all transformations begin in darkness. Think of a seed in the soil, a butterfly in its cocoon, or an infant in the womb.

And just like a seed, it needs the rain as much as it needs the sun in order to become what it is meant to be.

No. 123

Be more loving.

Behind every pair of folded arms is a heart that needs love. Behind every furrowed brow is a mind that needs understanding. We develop varieties of denial to protect our esteem, but at the core, we're all the same: Our eyes sparkle and our voices shake when we talk about family.

We feel compelled to lend a hand when we see a fellow peer struggle. We all feel homesick when we're busy in faraway lands for too long. We all feel melancholic when a certain smell brings us back to childhood. At the very core, we all want to be nurtured.

Love infuses values. It makes you a better person—not by asking, but by inspiring. We need love because we are vulnerable by default. We suffer easily (and inevitably); we need love to ameliorate unnecessary amounts of this suffering.

No. 124

Attitude matters more than the failure itself.

Failure will never not suck, it's your attitude towards it that makes it suck.

Growth, in concept, is easy—find a hurdle, jump over it, realize you can do more, repeat. If you fall, you try again. The thing is, every fall includes a punch to the ego. Failing means scarring: Pain repels you. You start predicting and fearing pain, then you stop trying altogether. Because if you never try, you'll never fail. But if you stop trying, your world shrinks.

Opportunities wither.

Curiosity dims.

Ambition dies.

Dreams blur into nothing but a faint memory. There are those who let that happen and those who realize that ego bruises aren't fatal wounds, and that success is more about allowing mistakes than knowing answers. Then you'll shed your fear and fail better.

You'll prove to yourself that you can survive anything.

No. 125

Keep moving.

Everyone agrees that stagnation causes decay and that it's good to keep moving.

But some people move forward eyeing what they can have while others keep looking back on what they had to leave behind. Some are pulled by will, others are running away from regret.

The people I usually think of as successful seem to be comfortable with moving in seasons: There's a time for everything and once the appropriate season has passed, they move on. Doing what is "right" is context-dependent. It's only right if it's done in the right time. We say it's good to keep moving, but we tend to forget that the bigger picture is also changing at its own providential pace—when you look at it this way, it really only makes sense to focus on the options of our current season.

Reach for the future, don't run from the past.

No. 126

Control your emotions.

Emotional control is the most important skill you can develop in your teenage years and early adulthood. If your emotions aren't on a leash, you're on *its* leash. You'll lose once-in-a-lifetime connections because you messed up the first impression. You'll destroy years of friendship in seconds. You'll say things you can't take back and do things you might spend the rest of your days regretting. Decisions made in intense emotions are typically rash and pushed by a desire to overpower instead of communicate.

The world is very small and burnt bridges can't be built back up; don't let emotional possession take a temporary spotlight that would cost you an important possibility.

No. 127

Learn from trial and error.

Everyone wants life hacks and advice from those that they consider to have 'made it' but the best hacks are the ones you develop yourself. Life is a single player game. No one sees reality from your perspective. Some lessons can't be learned secondhand, you have to feel it out.

No. 128

Never go to bed angry.

Every morning is the start of a new day, and every new day is a grace drawn forth from nothing. Every new day is a gift—why spoil it by carrying foul feelings over from the day before? Grudges make you suffer more than necessary, there's zero upside.

No. 129

Get out of your own way.

Insecurity kills dreams more than failure ever will. You know your vulnerabilities. You know how to hack your own defenses. You know exactly what to hold against yourself. And you know that you can actually succeed if you stop thinking about it and just get out of your own way.

No. 130

Don't be afraid of going first.

Everybody wants to dance; nobody wants to go first. You'll never miss a party if you're the host. Don't be afraid of making the first move; oftentimes, the people around you want the same thing. It takes one "let's do it" to start the fun in a group of "I'm fine with anything."

No. 131

Make haste slowly (*festina lente*).

Be urgent but don't rush. Be busy but not anxious. Move quickly but steadily. Compete with your past self, not time. Think long-term but take reachable steps. Have big dreams but make sound plans. Head in the sky, feet on the ground.

No. 132

Do not tolerate disrespect.

People will treat you the way you allow them too. What you're willing to tolerate is a confession of your character. Not setting boundaries is just another expression of people-pleasing.

No one is capable of reading minds. Communicate your needs, don't just keep them in your head.

No. 133

Be the bigger person.

Being the bigger person is about humility. Overheard gossip? Let it pass. Got into an argument? Dissolve it with some humor. Wronged by someone? Forgive them. Overlook the rough edges because there's zero gain in imposing their standards on other people.

You might be someone who never gossips or argues over petty, but that doesn't mean others won't. You might be more considerate than most, but that doesn't stop others from practicing bad habits.

Most importantly, your judgement of others is simultaneously a confession of your own character. Let them gossip. Let them squabble. You can be bigger than that by not taking any of it to heart.

Because being able to truly forgive or others requires the understanding that you are just as human. Just as fallible. And when you do wrong, you're just as in need of forgiveness as them.

No. 134

Entertain the possibility of alternatives.

There's more than one way to do something.

You have your way, and it's only one of many. Solutions often aren't found through struggling for control, but by giving way to possibilities. In hindsight, many 'problems' weren't problems at all, they were just part of the journey.

Don't confuse any stage of the exploration for a final destination. Weave what you learn into your tapestry of experience. Plans can be easily defeated by change, so learn to swim when the boat sinks.

No. 135

Be patient.

Almost every language has its own rendition of the saying 'good things take time'.

There's a universal appreciation for quality (over quantity) and an unspoken premium placed on beauty. We'd rather something take its time than have it be completed with lousy shortcuts. Are we perfectionists by instinct? Not necessarily. But the standards for making things beautiful is certainly linked to integrity, or something morally good. The need for intangible qualities like integrity, honesty, and diligence are deeply valued across cultures (which only show in high-quality work. Things done hastily are more associated with cheapness or carelessness).

No. 136

Deep clean your house.

Deep cleaning the house is therapeutic because you dig up things you thought you had forgotten. The pencil case you used everyday in high school. Old birthday cards from friends who now live in other cities.

Your mind is the same; memories are never truly forgotten. Often, your head feels fuzzy and cluttered not because there's "too much", but because the things inside aren't recognized, organized, or integrated.

The purpose of deep cleaning is to purge, reorganize, and integrate. Get rid of what's no longer good. Repurpose idle objects that are meaninglessly taking up space. Order things in a way that makes your life easier. When you know where everything is and why they're important to you, your house and your mind no longer feel cluttered.

No. 137

Ask for advice from the right kind of people.

Just like how you have to hold a book at a proper distance in order to read the words, there's a certain separation that's required between you and the person you're asking for help: Loved ones who are too close may want the best for you but their judgement can be blurred by emotional intimacy, or they don't want to hurt you. A total stranger may have good experience but can be too far away to know anything about you to tailor their advice to you personally.

When in doubt, ask people of different distances. Adjust the advice you receive to be as objectively accurate as possible by hearing from people who read you differently.

No. 138

Learn how to break bad news.

Being able to deliver bad news and hard truths gracefully is the ultimate hallmark of wisdom.

Someone who can say unpleasant things without damaging relationships must've truly grasped what it means to want the best for the ones they care for.

The thing is, people have a stubborn tendency to hear what they want to hear and find external things to blame, so even when it's a close friend who's making the tough judgements, it's hard not to build up walls and rationalize the truth in what they're saying about you.

No. 139

Stay persistent.

You've got the dreams, the dedication, and the thick skin—now what? Why is the magic still not happening? Sometimes we forget about the importance of patience and the power of compounding.

Given enough time, water droplets can break through stone. Rome wasn't built in a day. If what you're doing is truly great, then it won't be easy. It has to start small. It needs time and room to grow. It needs consistent nourishment and protection.

There's a certain point where things are no longer in your control—do what you can, then stand back and let it grow.

No. 140

Embrace aging.

Aging is a common fear and saying that it's "just a fact of life" doesn't make anyone feel better. But I think the silver lining to aging is that it keeps us humble. We aren't meant to live forever, nor should we, and if we didn't age I doubt we'd treasure life the way we do.

Aging is the reason why we have to learn from our mistakes. As we get older, we have less time to correct ourselves and recover from adversity. Take your health seriously, practice dealing with people, and prize your resilience.

Aging is the accumulation of wisdom. Like rings in a tree, new layers never disappear as they are replaced, they only move closer to the core.

No. 141

Read more books.

Books are proof that our ancestors cared about us. To pass hard-won information through the centuries, generations have been taught to read and write. A collective mythos has been conceived, protected, fortified, glorified, banned, burned, and resurrected—again and again. All for us.

No. 142

Show yourself more gratitude.

There's a common sentiment in hustle culture about how people are too soft on themselves and everyone should try harder with blood sweat and tears.

But I often think that the opposite is true. I think people can be too hard on themselves sometimes without realizing it: When was the last time you felt proud of your work? Do you end each day counting the moments you felt appreciative of what you're capable of?

Ambition is good, but is your act of perpetual self-betterment done out of spite or respect for yourself? Don't forget to show gratitude to yourself—you deserve to be thanked, congratulated, and encouraged as much as others.

This is how you make your work fulfilling, because what feels remarkable to you will become worthy in the eyes of other people.

No. 143

Distinguish what you want from what you think you want.

When I left corporate the biggest mental block I had to work through was separating what I *wanted* to do versus what I felt like I *ought* to do.

I learned to separate social expectations from intuitions that were hard to describe with words. I learned that if you blindly follow oughts and ignore wants, your identity will stray further away from your true sense of self.

But ignored wants don't go away, in fact, they amplify. The greater this misalignment gets, the harder it is to enjoy yourself or find yourself likeable.

No. 144

Pay attention to your intuition.

The difference between intuition and wishful thinking is that intuition should make you feel slightly anxious.

Plain fantasies will never make you feel uncomfortable. But intuition is more potent than imagination and daydreams; intuition is a feeling that demands action. It makes you anxious because it's not a fleeting fantasy—it's an idea waiting to be executed into reality. It's daunting because it demands courage. It makes you think instead of dream because it makes you aware that you're actually able to accomplish it if you gave it a chance.

No. 145

Make the situation you're in as fun as possible.

Kids have this instinct to make every situation they're in as fun as possible. Sharing snacks, telling stories, asking questions that are simple but not easy to explain, letting their curiosity latch onto whatever feels creative—this is the wonder we ought to preserve as we age.

No. 146

Strike a balance between guidance and freedom.

Give children cardinal values and let them do with it what they will.

When we tell children to 'follow the rules', what we're actually trying to do is save them from the trouble of having to deal with the consequences of transgressing social or cultural norms. Obedience is one thing, but the underlying motivation for teaching such obedience is so that they can avoid social-cultural punishment and ostracism. In other words, we want to save our children from suffering, because the fate of a pariah is irredeemably lonely.

After all, isn't that what love is? Saving each other from preventable and unnecessary amounts of suffering?

The key word in this definition of love is "unnecessary", because suffering, aggregately speaking, is unpreventable.

If we are to have free will, we must be fallible. Suffering is the promise that we have the volition and ability to change our circumstances, for better or for worse. Nested in free will is the possibility of both humiliating failure and glorious success.

As C. S. Lewis once said, "Try to exclude the possibility of suffering which the order of nature and the existence of free-wills involve, and you find that you have excluded life itself."

No. 147

Judge your day by what you've created, not what you've consumed.

Creation is an active process, consumption is passive. Creation demands more of you—it's a willful exercise of your ability to reflect, question, and think critically. And this tells you a lot more about yourself.

A large part of creativity isn't the thinking, it's the incubating. Creative work is the sweet wine of fermented thoughts—much of my eurekas today come from ideas that were planted a long time ago. I can tell a lot more about my mental state by its daily outputs than inputs.

No. 148

Apologize to heal, not compensate.

A "narcissist's apology" describes when someone apologizes to make themselves feel better for what they did. Instead of saying "I'm sorry for what I did", it usually sounds something like "I'm sorry that you feel that way, but [self-defensive rationalization]."

The purpose of apologizing is to heal, not compensate. The person you're apologizing to has been hurt, not wronged. "Facts don't care about your feelings" is not completely true when it comes to people you love and care about. When nurturing people emotionally, feelings are part of the facts.

No. 149

Make your own heaven.

Heaven is a very real place on Earth, but it only happens in moments. Times like laughing with your friends until your abs hurt, drinking water on a hot day when you're parched, eating homemade meals after living abroad, or listening to songs from a favorite summer.

Heaven is what we call the feeling of an overflow of joy. Being able to capture happiness in the moment is a choice, and being able to cultivate good habits of remembering these moments is a skill.

What we choose to take away from our experience makes our existence a paradise.

No. 150

Embrace adversity.

Without storms, we wouldn't grow roots that are strong enough to reach the womb of the earth. Without sunshine, we wouldn't grow vines and branches long enough to reach the sky. Both are needed; the taller we grow, the deeper we need to be in the ground.

This is our balance.

No. 151

Don't take things personally.

The first step to taking things less personally is remembering that people don't see things as things are, they see it the way they are. For example, someone who looks for a reason to complain will always find it—someone else's thought patterns do not indicate your character.

No. 152

Find your purpose.

Everyone needs something that makes waking up in the morning feel like a privilege instead of a chore. Something that makes the day feel like a gift instead of a burden. Something that tickles their ambition like a flicker at a candle's wick. It's what makes it all feel worth it.

No. 153

Learning is not equal to understanding.

Understanding something is existential, not intellectual.

Theory only becomes useful when it is crystallized in practice. You can pass tests and complete degrees. You can be full of theory. But do you know what to do with that knowledge? How it matters and why? The best philosophy is lived, not talked about.

Students who are good at tests are good at learning, but they might not be good at mastering.

They're good at gaining knowledge, but they might not be good at knowing what to do with that knowledge.

Some people win on paper, some win in real life. This is the only way dreams become reality.

No. 154

Stop blaming your parents.

J. K. Rowling once said, "There is an expiry date on blaming your parents for steering you in the wrong direction; the moment you are old enough to take the wheel, responsibility lies with you."

We don't get to choose the hand we're dealt but we get to play it to our advantage. Circumstances can make or break us depending on what we do about it, and there comes a day we have to cut the psychological umbilical cord, or, mental ties like blaming your parents for who you are. Otherwise, we are never truly independent.

To be independent means being able to succeed, but also being able to fail. Realizing that we are fragile is only the first step.

Next, we must grasp that what we achieve inwardly will change outer reality. Thoughts influence destiny.

No. 155

Slow down.

This may sound counterintuitive, but the only way to get out of a rut is by slowing down instead of speeding up or fighting against it by doing more.

Sand is best held with an open palm, the tighter your grip the more the grains fall through your fingers.

Be relaxed.

Find steadiness and peace.

No. 156

Forgive yourself as you would a neighbor.

The reason why it's harder to forgive ourselves (than others) is because we are excruciatingly self-conscious of our own inadequacies.

We know who we are when no one's watching. It's easy to self-blame because we have nowhere to hide our imperfections from our own judgement.

The person you've known for the longest is yourself. Why is it so hard to see the best in that person, someone who's managed to survive the worst? Why is it so hard to show compassion to that person, someone whose success and joy you benefit from the most?

We are morally inclined to 'be a good person'—most of us would do what is best for our loved ones without batting an eye. As a result, we give more grace to others than ourselves, when in reality, we are just as worthy as those we care about.

No. 157

See people for who they are, not who you think they are.

The easiest way to become instantly happier is by not imposing your standards on other people.

Don't try to change others into who you want them to be—sometimes, we like our own expectations of someone more than who they actually are.

No. 158

Don't bury your emotions.

If you don't deal with your emotions your emotions will deal with you.

Ignored feelings never die, they come back in uglier forms and when least expected.

Maturity is making peace with turbulent memories so they don't visit the present in harmful ways.

As the saying goes, if you don't heal what hurt you, you'll bleed on people who didn't cut you.

No. 159

Be silent to hear your intuition.

A lot of people have been told growing up that they're too sensitive, and overtime learned to "toughen up" only to realize that heightened sensitivity is their greatest gift.

Learned toughness and an armor of logic distract us from the gut intuition we look for. Somewhere along the way, "listen to your guts" became just a cliche. We've all adopted a rational, checklist style way of thinking. We fill the resume. That's why so many decisions can check the boxes and be correct on paper but still don't *feel* right.

What's correct isn't always what's true.

All we want is to be able to clearly hear our intuition again. Rationale used to save us from impulse, but when swung too far in the opposite way, rationale becomes an intuition blocker.

The core of a lot of self-help psychology is just about increasing that sensitivity again and doing what *feels* right. Being still and silent helps us quiet our brains so we can tune into the whispers of gut feelings.

No. 160

Self-stewardship is better than self-care.

Wanting the best for yourself is no easy task, even though it's obvious.

That's because what's good isn't always what feel nice.

It doesn't feel nice for a couch potato to start hitting the gym. It doesn't feel nice to receive reality checks.

True self-care is self-stewardship.

To steward yourself means being responsible for your own wellness and choosing what's best even if the best doesn't feel comfortable. Sometimes I ask myself "if someone assigned me to take care of Sherry for the next 70-80 years, would I say I'm doing a good job?"

No. 161

Have some courage.

You have all the information and advice you need. Most times, you already know the answer. Everything on top of what you already believe in is just consolation.

But you don't need other heads to nod at what you already know is right—all that's left is courage.

You are the only person you can't hide the truth from when you mess up. When you know what you want, no amount of external affirmation is going to substitute the kinetic energy that only courage can provide to turn a vision into reality.

All that's left is guts and action.

No. 162

Practice love.

My favorite take on love comes from Erich
Fromm, something like: love is a practice, a
habit, a discipline. It takes intention and effort.
That's why you can judge how well someone
can love by how they love themselves. It's not
about one thing or person, it's a capacity. An
ability.

No. 163

Find a good therapist.

Viktor Frankl might have the best perspective on therapy:

A good therapist should be like an ophthalmologist, not a painter. They should help you see the world as it really is, not as the picture of the world they've created themselves.

A second opinion is not always good for clarity.

No. 164

Overcome discouragement.

How you face discouragement determines everything.

You've made it this far—did you bring yourself all the way here just to abandon it all? You're not called to conquer the world, just your own doubts. There's nothing between you and what you want except action and hesitation; some people hit one disappointment and think it's the arrival, some only see it as a plateau before the next resurrection.

A destination is only final if you say it is, otherwise, it's just another pit stop for you to rest, reflect, and decide: to keep climbing or quit.

No. 165

Focus on who you can become, not just who you are now.

Some people only remember the past from a first-person perspective. Others can recall what happened from both first- and third-person.

 This makes all the difference: when you can see yourself from the third-person perspective, you realize you aren't just a character in the grand narrative—you're also the author. You aren't just aware of who you used to be, you're also aware of who you can become.

As Aldous Huxley puts it, "experience is not what happens to you; it's what you do with what happens to you."

The world is an arena in which our actions and sense of limitation are reflexive.

The more we test how malleable it is, the more we are capable of changing it.

No. 166

Decide slowly, act quickly.

Decision anxiety wears us out more than the actual workload.

Most of the time, when we fear the future, what we actually fear is not being able to control it. We're scared that if we make the wrong decision, any bad result will be entirely our fault.

That's why slowness is key—If the future is the result of a collection of decisions, then taking the time to make each decision carefully will alleviate a lot of the fear associated with tomorrow's unknowns.

Direction is more important than speed.

Take your time when needed: decide slowly, act quickly.

No. 167

Be softer with one another.

Most unnecessary conflicts can be avoided if both parties can hold their opinions a little looser and observe the situation from afar:

Look instead of see.

Listen instead of hear.

Feel instead of touch.

Less thinking, more appreciation.

Less rationalizing, more living.

No. 168

Think more about other people.

Confidence and humility are paired.

People who are confident don't feel like they have to prove themselves all the time—they think less about themselves without thinking less of themselves.

They assume they're not the smartest, that everyone they meet knows something they don't.

As the saying goes, "humility is not thinking less of yourself, but thinking of yourself less."

No. 169

Appreciate solitude.

Enjoy periods of isolation and solitude. It's an important practice, especially for creative people.

The mimetic mind needs intermittent fasting. How could you come up with something new, innovative, and different if you're thinking the same as everyone else?

Let your ideas evolve like Darwin's finches. The more separated you are from the crowd, the more unique and exotic your mind becomes.

If you want to stand out, grow alone for a while. If you want to be innovative, think alone for a while. If you want to be novel, work alone for a while.

Let what grows inside stay inside. Let it ferment and see where things go.

No. 170

Have a sense of humor.

Humor is an interesting thing it's like, "if I can make you laugh, you'll actually take me a bit more seriously".

The ability to make light of a situation is a sign of wisdom. The sillier you can be, the deeper you understand the nuances of human emotions. Humor can get to the truth faster and more frictionless than logic and rational persuasion. Having a good sense of humor or being able to laugh things off boils down to humility.

Sometimes, it's better to not take yourself too seriously.

At the end of the day, we all just want to have fun.

No. 171

Stop procrastinating.

Put the book down.

ABOUT THE AUTHOR

Hi, I'm Sherry. I write about human nature, purposeful living, and creativity. I believe that the key to personal freedom and happiness is having a clear mind, an optimistic heart, and a grateful soul.

I write on Twitter (@SchrodingrsBrat) and blog.theplurisociety.com.

Feel free to reach out on either of the platforms! ☺

Thank you for reading.

theplurisociety.com

Made in the USA
Middletown, DE
30 August 2023